baby rooms

Heidi Tyline King

BONNIER
BOOKS

BONNIER BOOKS

This edition published by Bonnier Books,
Appledram Barns, Birdham Road, Chichester,
West Sussex PO20 7 EQ, UK
www.bonnierbooks.co.uk

WELDON OWEN GROUP
Chief Executive Officer **John Owen**
Chief Financial Officer **Simon Fraser**

WELDON OWEN INC.
Chief Executive Officer and President **Terry Newell**
Senior VP, International Sales **Stuart Laurence**
VP, Sales and Marketing **Amy Kaneko**

VP, Creative Director **Gaye Allen**
Senior Art Director **Emma Boys**
Designers **Anna Giladi** and **Diana Heom**

VP, Publisher **Roger Shaw**
Executive Editor **Elizabeth Dougherty**
Managing Editor **Karen Templer**
Project Editor **Veronica Peterson**
Editorial Assistant **Sarah Gurman**

Production Director **Chris Hemesath**
Production Manager **Michelle Duggan**
Colour Manager **Teri Bell**

A WELDON OWEN PRODUCTION
Copyright © 2008 Weldon Owen Inc.

ISBN: 978-1-905825-54-7

10 9 8 7 6 5 4 3 2 1

Printed in China.

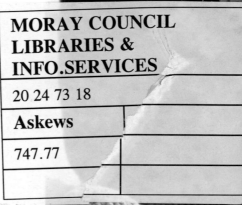

contents

the new nursery

There was a time when decorating a nursery meant a simple choice of which pastel: blue for a boy, pink for a girl, and yellow or green if you were waiting to find out. Perhaps a child-oriented theme factored in—teddy bears or balloons, for example. Today the colour and decorating options are endless, as it's much more common for the style of a nursery to reflect the rest of the home and the parents' personalities. As you start to plan your baby's nursery, the number of possibilities might seem both exciting and a little daunting.

Fortunately, being pregnant or preparing for an adoption provides built-in nesting time to prepare to welcome your family's newest member into your life—and your home. Let your imagination take flight as you page through this book for ideas, and use the checklist on the following page to organise the tasks of planning, furnishing and decorating rooms for your baby.

Start by thinking about the space you have available for a nursery and choosing a colour scheme and style that appeal to you. Also consider ways to incorporate your own personal flair. Contemporary nursery colour combinations, for instance, range from bold saturated colours, such as purples and oranges, to versatile neutral palettes, such as creams and warm wood tones.

You'll also want to prepare the rest of your house. You might want a downstairs changing station or a dedicated play space. Maybe you'd like to set up a small cot next to the bed in your room. A comfortable chair is key at first when feeding an infant, and later a kid-friendly kitchen will come into play.

Above all, the tips and tricks featured here are tried-and-true, gleaned from homes around the world. Let them inspire you as you create the nursery of your dreams.

getting organised

The more you can do while you are expecting, the less you will have to juggle once your baby arrives. Here's a checklist of essentials to help you get organised.

the basics

paint or wallpaper This is a big decision: be sure to test swatches

wall decorations Anything from murals to masterpieces

lighting Install a dimmer to the overhead light and add a task lamp

flooring Put non-slip pads under all rugs

babyproofing Consult books or online for a home-safety checklist

shelves Great for holding books and baskets of toys; anchor to wall

other storage Baskets, boxes or caddies for toys, books and extra clothes

sweet dreams

cot Assemble and verify sturdiness

cot mattress Must fit firmly into cot

mobile Remove when your baby can push up on hands and knees

bumpers If used, tie tightly; remove when your baby can push up on hands and knees

linens At least three fitted sheets and waterproof pads

basket Preferably one that lifts out of its base

window treatments Room-darkening ones, such as blackout or multitiered curtains

well fed

comfortable chair Rocking chair or whatever chair works best for you

footstool Nursing stool or ottoman

cushions Nursing cushion and other types of cushions as needed

high chair Look for an easy-to-fasten harness, one-handed tray release and adjustable height

drop cloth For under the high chair, piece of plastic cloth cut to size or a plastic tablecloth

change of pace

dresser Place in closet or use top to hold changing pad

drawer organisers Great for sorting small items such as hats, socks or toiletries

changing table Look for one with orderly storage and potential for other future uses

changing pad Water resistant with upturned sides and strap

nappy pail Consider the cost of special refill bags before choosing

laundry hamper Plus washable liners

bath time

infant bathtub For the early months, look for one with a non-slip surface and a stopper

bath seat A later purchase, for a baby who can sit up unassisted

bath toy container One that lets toys dry, such as a mesh bag or a large plastic colander

tap covers To add soft padding over bathroom hardware

scald valve For the bathtub, to prevent accidental burns

toiletry container Keep all toiletries in one place to make bathing easier

extras

music A CD player or other stereo system

baby monitor Add batteries if needed and test for static

knobs Replace knobs on furniture, such as dressers, for an easy personalised look

growth chart Track just how fast your little one grows

mirror There's nothing quite like a familiar face to calm a baby

friendly advice Have a friend who's a parent "test drive" your nursery

first steps

Planning a nursery begins with two key decisions: style and colour. Once you know you want a modern nursery with a palette of brights or a more traditional room with warm neutrals (among countless options), the furnishings and other choices will naturally follow.

set the scene

Practical considerations abound when planning a nursery. Start by tackling the basic surroundings and safety issues before shifting your focus to decorating.

design time

Rather than rushing in to decorate, give yourself time to think through what you need and want in a nursery. Your second trimester is the perfect time to begin lists and sketches, especially if you plan to find out the gender of your child.

all about colour

Modern nursery palettes range from soft neutrals to bold saturated colours. Pick any combination of hues that makes you happy, keeping in mind how the colours of large surfaces—the walls, the floor and furniture—will interact with each other.

chosen style

Contemporary children's spaces tend to reflect the rest of the house, so consider your home's overall look when picking a style for the nursery. Also keep in mind that a sophisticated approach ages better than an infant-oriented one.

right light

Outfit your nursery with soft lighting to ease any nappy changes at night or transitions from your arms to the cot. Install a dimmer on overhead lighting, and place lamps near the changing table and chair, but out of reach of your baby.

air care

Good ventilation is important for a healthy nursery environment. Open the windows for fresh air as often as possible, and consider installing a ceiling fan for increased circulation. This is also a good time to change boiler filters.

safety first

Babyproofing needs will evolve as your baby gains mobility. Start now by getting down on the floor and looking around from her perspective. Anchor furniture, pad any sharp edges and install safety latches and baby gates wherever needed.

orange crush

Hip and lively, orange is a refreshing choice. This bold room avoids being brash with a white cot and rocking chair to counter the walls' intensity.

pattern pizzazz

If you're waiting to find out your baby's gender, start with neutrals, such as haystack yellow bedding, and later personalise with accessories. Pink pillows (left) announce "It's a girl!"

use cot placement to both define spaces and direct traffic flow

In a nursery roomy enough for two, parallel white cots create a shared play area, which also provides space between sleeping babies. Placing the head of each cot against a wall provides the advantage of access on three sides. While doubled furnishings are identical, securely anchored photos proclaim who's who.

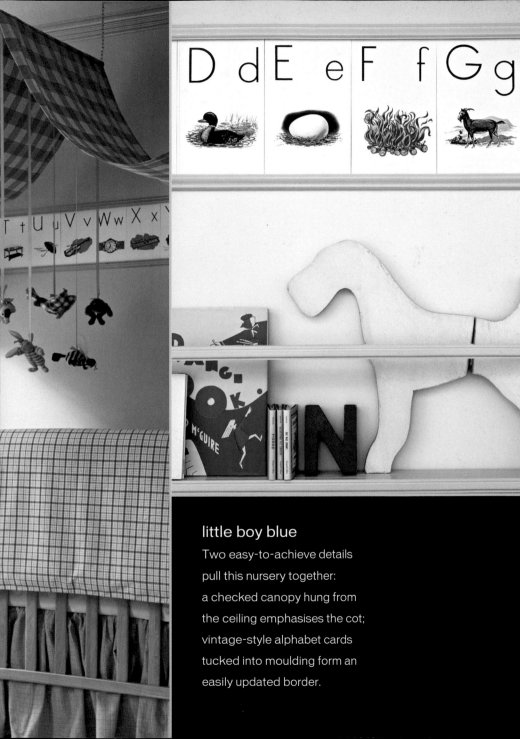

little boy blue

Two easy-to-achieve details
pull this nursery together:
a checked canopy hung from
the ceiling emphasises the cot;
vintage-style alphabet cards
tucked into moulding form an
easily updated border.

wood and cotton create a natural space for a baby

The warm woods found in this intentionally spare nursery lend it a timeless feel. A changing mat, baby clothes and toiletries are tucked behind doors and into drawers in the built-in armoire, leaving a wicker rocking horse and the cot as the room's focal points. The toy boat and bed linens provide spots of colour.

letter perfect

Photo transfers of a sky inspired the tonal palette of this nursery. Lower case letters stencilled in shades of blue are an easy way to customise drawers.

speak softly Pale green walls or linens paired with glossy white wood look
smart in a unisex nursery. Pegs and a fabric armoire offer clothes-storage options.

bold and bright This green-and-white silhouetted nature scene is so striking that the room needs little else. Streamlined wood furniture keeps the look clean.

bright ideas

A nursery requires certain essentials–a cot, a changing table, storage–but once these needs are met, the fun of decorating awaits. From mobiles to murals, creative finishing touches will make your baby's space special while reflecting your own style and personality.

make it special

Think about the places where you enjoy spending time. What makes them special? See if you can adapt these details to make your baby's room feel as welcoming.

patterns first

A practical decorating approach is to start with fabric—the bedding and window treatments—or the rug, especially with patterns. Paint, which is where most people begin, is the easiest to match, so you can pick it at a later stage.

on the wall

Paint and wallpaper are both great ways to add colour and/or pattern to walls. Shop for finishes that wipe clean with ease. Test large swatches on a wall before committing to a roomful of anything. Tape off stripes or use stencils to add interest.

artistic flair

Artwork is as important in the nursery as anywhere else in the house. Choose it with an open mind: a quilt, a poster of a Cubist or Impressionist work or even original art might complement the room's style perfectly. Anchor each item securely.

creative mobiles

A nursery staple, a mobile offers an opportunity to entertain your little one and to play up the room's decor with assorted colours and shapes. Hang one over the cot but out of reach. Remove it when your baby starts to push up on hands and knees.

all in the family

Displaying toys or photos from your own childhood on a shelf or in a framed box adds instant personal appeal to a nursery. Keep up the family connection by adding mementos from your baby, such as first shoes or a dressy outfit, to the collection.

my space

Babies love to look at baby faces, making the nursery an ideal place to display photos of your child. Use a growth chart to mark just how rapidly your little one is sprouting and alphabet letters or a sign to spell out exactly whose room it is.

a classic combination
of red and blue takes
an imaginative detour

To add drama to any room,
including a nursery, think
trompe l'oeil–French for
"tricks the eye." A palace
mural covers three walls
of this nursery, giving it an
exotic feel. Striped Roman
shades reflect the mural's
colour and mood. A graphic
red-and-white pattern, blue
walls and a chic cot ground
things in the here and now.

a room with a view

The rocking chair and dresser are quirky yet classic, with clean lines that hold their own against the bold backdrop. The chair's position in the room gives parents the benefit of the apartment's city views.

graphic appeal Make a statement with a full-size mural that ties together related patterns (above) or by papering an accent wall in bold stripes (right).

around we go

Shades of orange and peachy pinks are creatively combined here—note the way they alternate on the walls and ceiling, around the "rickrack" border. A glossy white floor and cot set off the colours. Circles, orbs and ovals are a recurring motif.

hang time Anchor a colourful quilt or large piece of artwork to the wall. These fluttering butterflies complement the art, in a palette that works for a boy or a girl.

matched set

Derived from the charming animal-print fabric used for the pouffe, a soft wall hanging and a window shade, spots of pink and mint green punctuate this yellow-and-white nursery.

inspiring objects

A knit green-and-blue blanket captures this nursery's palette. To personalise furniture, replace its hardware; here the knobs on the dresser reflect the nursery's wall colour.

now and later A neutral backdrop works for a child of any age. An out-of-reach shelf and clips on a wire safely display treasures, which can easily be changed.

plan ahead Brightly coloured graphics and decorative accents meant for kids will also appeal to babies, and can be grown into rather than needing to be updated.

checkmate

Gingham softens primary colours and adds country charm. This nursery uses the print generously for throw pillows, window treatments and other decorative elements.

tall tales Track your child's development with a yardstick growth chart, or make a space-saving, scaled-down version. Include photos and ages along with heights.

show off Keep treasured pieces close. A fabric-lined case cradles special baby shoes and a finger puppet (above); a hand-knit red outfit brightens a nursery (right).

sleeping

A peacefully sleeping child is a joy in many ways. For one thing, that time offers a chance for you to rest or tend to other matters. Style, safety and practicality are all factors to consider when selecting a cot and creating a space where your baby can sleep comfortably.

get some rest

Darling as a baby is, you will want to curb night-time meetings by making sleeping quarters as cosy as possible, leading to sweet dreams for both of you.

good buy

Cot access and stability are even more important than style considerations. Shake a cot to evaluate sturdiness, then confirm that the rail slides up and down quietly and with ease. Look for smooth or covered corners, secure slats and locking casters.

safety check

Hand-me-downs are often welcome, but be sure to check that cots, baskets, cradles and other baby items meet current safety standards. You can find up-to-date guidelines, manufacturer recalls and evolving industry standards online.

cot notes

To ensure safe cot placement, situate it so your baby can't pull down anything, such as lamps or curtains, and avoid placing it under a shelf or anything heavy that could fall. Artwork and other wall hangings should be well anchored to the wall.

good night room

Window treatments are an easy way to dress up a room, but make sure that whatever you choose is room-darkening to help your baby sleep. Roller shades, blackout fabric and multi-tiered curtains offer levels of control over incoming light.

pillow talk

For stylistic reasons, cots are photographed quite often with blankets, pillows, dolls and soft toys in them. In reality, a cot should be empty to eliminate any danger of suffocation. Likewise, dressing a baby in layers is safer than a blanket.

muffle sounds

White noise can keep a baby sleeping peacefully while you are up and about. The sound of a fan or soft music can soothe while muffling noise. (The sound of running water, a hair-drier or a vacuum cleaner helps some babies go to sleep.)

light lifting

When twins arrive, portability is a major consideration. These wicker baskets lift off their stands, making it easy to move a waking baby away from one who is still asleep.

baby makes three

Welcome your infant into your life by integrating a small cot and a rocking chair into your bedroom. Look at options that attach to the bed or fit snugly beside it, offering quick and easy access when it's time for a midnight feed. When you're ready, you can move him to a full-size cot in his own room.

neutral territory All-natural materials give this nursery a cohesive look. The canvas-and-wood cot is perfectly sized for an infant and can be rolled anywhere.

in vogue One unique piece of furniture, such as this iron cot, can up the style quotient of a room. The securely tied bumper goes all the way up to the top.

so high

Look for a cot with an adjustable mattress height. Positioning the mattress higher eases picking up or laying down an infant. When your baby starts to pull up, lower the mattress.

round off This oval cot is as practical as it is attractive, eliminating sharp corners. Its curves are echoed in other elements of the room, including the mobile.

day and night

The elegant tiebacks on these two-toned curtains suggest an unveiling: in this case, a cottage-inspired cot smartly moved out of reach of the window and the curtains.

centre stage

The cot is a nursery's raison d'être—if space allows, like in this nursery, showcase it in the middle of the room.

room to grow

Plan for the inevitable with a
design scheme that can grow
with your child. Soft rugs and
colourful accessories, such as
knitted flags, work for all ages,
while the cot converts and
extends into a toddler bed.

double duty

An heirloom basket is so
perfectly at home in this
serene bedroom—with
its embrace of all things
reclaimed—that it's been
granted a new role now that
the baby has outgrown it.

playing

The best playrooms are stimulating and interactive, full of books and toys to nurture a child's interests and development. But to create a safe and inviting space for play, you'll need to think beyond just the toys—to matters of display, storage and comfort.

have a little fun

Little one, little one, what do you see? Considering a play space from your baby's viewpoint provides insight into how best to furnish, decorate and arrange it.

intrepid explorer

Since the whole world is new, it doesn't take much to occupy an infant—a few toys on a blanket will do. But once mobile, your baby will be eager to explore. Be ready with a babyproofed space in your home arranged so that nothing is off-limits.

underfoot

Crawling babies become well acquainted with the floor. Rugs or carpets that are stain-resistant and easy on the knees are good choices, as is low-maintenance wood or laminate flooring. Be sure to secure all rugs with non-slip pads.

in storage

When storing playthings, group "like with like" in containers scaled to their contents, such as fabric bins for soft toys, baskets for board books or felt bags for blocks. Labels, especially with pictures, will guide things back to their homes.

give the word

Letters and words are well-loved inspirations for decorating play spaces. Space parallel mouldings on a wall to hold a border of alphabet cards, paint pictures on the wall and label them, or mount colourful magnetic boards with jumbo letters.

in the zone

Teachers often section classrooms into zones for different activities. This plan also makes sense at home. Group low shelves of books near reading chairs. Put musical toys in one corner, trains in another. Later, add a space for craft supplies.

age range

To help accommodate children of different ages in a playroom, use tall bookcases anchored to the wall. Store older children's toys, games and art supplies on upper shelves, out of the reach of anyone not old enough to play with them.

discovery zone

Accessories and activities that stimulate sight, touch and hearing give baby a compelling place of her own. A bookshelf next to a reading chair lends itself to impromptu story time.

play mates

Magnetic boards add colour in this play space, as do the metal buckets being used to organise small toys. The buckets' fabric liners can be removed for easy washing. Letters offer educational and decorative elements right from the start. Playing with jumbo ones provides babies with a tactile experience.

floor plan Satisfy your baby's curiosity by keeping things at her level: on the floor. Opt for soft textures, furniture without sharp corners and simple help-yourself bins.

cosy corner

There's no need to convert an entire room into a baby's play space. A corner of a room—defined by a rug, furnished with playthings and a chair for together time—is all a baby needs.

clear clutter As the collections of books and toys grow, so does the need to be organised. Baskets are indispensable, as are cabinets and drawers at kid level.

bulletin beauties

Colourful paper vignettes in
bookcase shelves dress up
ordinary furniture and add
personality to a room.

a place for everything Rows of wooden pegs arrange tiny puppets into a colourful display. A changing table finds new life as a storage shelf for soft toys.

playing nice

With furniture scaled for children, siblings of varying ages can share play space and storage. Lidded boxes are best for puzzles and other toys with multiple pieces, while open baskets unite soft toys.

feeding

Babies revel in the glorious discovery of food—indeed, it is among their first forays as individual explorers. For parents, the experience is more enjoyable—and even less messy—when you have anticipated your baby's needs and assembled all of the essential supplies.

get set for feeding

Keeping a baby fed is another one of those surprisingly time-consuming tasks. The right equipment, organised supplies and comfortable seating make it much easier.

take a seat

Typically, infants feed every two to three hours, making a comfortable chair for feeding sessions a must. While a nursing chair with a table is a popular choice, try out different chairs and footstools to find what works best for you.

extra comforts

Once you have a chair designated for feeding your infant, add a nursing pillow (whether nursing or bottle-feeding) and a cosy blanket for yourself. Both can play a part in the decor; for instance, a pillow cover can be made to match the cot linens.

at the ready

Designate a grab-and-go spot in your kitchen: a drawer, a cupboard shelf or a basket on a worktop. Stock it with essential feeding equipment—bibs, muslins, bottles (or cups), bowls, spoons—for convenient access when your baby is hungry.

sitting high

Choose a high chair with safety and ease of use foremost in mind. Test and make sure that the harness and tray are easy to secure and undo. Look for a solid middle bar, level legs and smooth washable surfaces (crevices attract crumbs).

clean sweep

High-chair mealtimes can be messy affairs. Place an easy-to-clean mat underneath to protect the floor. Available in many patterns, plastic cloth offers a stylish option. Have a piece cut to size at a fabric shop, or simply buy a tablecloth.

booster basics

When your child graduates to a booster seat, choose one that straps securely to the chair and has a sturdy harness. As with high chairs, plastic is great: you can simply wipe it down or give it a good wash in the sink.

rock-a-bye baby Equipping the nursery with a chair that's comfortable for feeding makes for a smooth transition from there to the changing table or the cot.

sweet spot Don't overlook your own comfort at feeding time. In addition to muslins, keep magazines, a blanket and a glass of water where you can reach them.

bedtime story

A day-bed allows new parents to curl up with their baby for feeds at any time of day or night. Supplies stored in handled baskets are easy to transport to anywhere in the house.

eating adventure
Make mealtime fun with colourful utensils and dishes. The space becomes uniquely yours with the addition of pictures and bright images under clear acrylic on the table.

stow away

Wire baskets with sturdy
handles create portable
storage that can be hidden
away or moved as needed.

family meal A high chair that blends into the kitchen decor helps its occupant feel more like part of the dining crowd. Some chairs even have adjustable heights.

name game Moving to a booster seat is an exciting development. Label chairs with each child's name—your littlest one will feel even more like one of the big kids.

changing

The frequency with which a baby must be changed, dressed or bathed can be comical. Streamline these routines with a well-ordered changing station combined with organised storage for the essentials—nappies and wipes, clothing and shoes, bath toys and toiletries.

dressed for success

With stylish, safe and organised accommodations, nappy changes, getting your little one dressed and bath time can be fun events rather than chores.

table it

If you're shopping for a ready-made changing table, look for one that can do duty later as a storage unit or dresser. You can also improvise a changing station by adding a mat on top of a dresser or a table that's a convenient height.

multiple choice

Assemble a few portable nappy-changing caddies and place them around the house, so that you will have the essentials handy as you and your baby move about. Include a roll-up mat, nappies, wipes, ointment and plastic bags for disposal.

fashion space

Consider consolidating clothes storage by placing the dresser in the wardrobe under a rail for hanging clothes, such as dresses. Place dividers or boxes inside dresser drawers to keep like items, such as tiny vests or socks, together.

all sorts

Establish a system for sorting and storing new and hand-me-down clothes by size and by season. Some people wash new clothes before storing them; others swear you should never take off a tag until your baby can wear that item.

not too hot

Set the temperature of your water heater to 49°C (120°F) or lower, and use a thermometer to check the temperature of hot water from the tap. When buying a baby bathtub, look for one with a non-slip surface and a stopper in the bottom.

take a seat

There are additional safety considerations when your baby starts to use a bath seat or to sit directly in the bath. Install padding around tap handles and a non-slip bath mat. If you travel frequently, an inflatable baby bath is a good buy.

August 16th
Heidi rolls over!

quick change

This modular changing unit is made to adapt. Its various parts can be used separately as needs evolve, or the unit can take on a new role in another room.

nappy central A mat-topped dresser and secure overhead shelf make up a complete nappy station. Red accents, including a stool, brighten the scene.

designer trick Arrange furniture, accessories and supplies in small vignettes. A framed set of mementos complements this cottage-style changing table.

simple solutions

S-hooks on a curtain rail organise items over a custom-painted changing station. Reflections in a mirror mounted on the wall offer a fun distraction.

case for space Baby clothes take up little hanging space. Make full use of a wardrobe by sliding in a chest of drawers for folded clothes and other supplies.

sort it out

Babies cycle as quickly through sizes as seasons. Keep up with the changes by sorting clothing into clear bins so you can see what's inside. Mark each with the size it contains.

artful adaptation

Incorporate baby furniture into your existing decor. A small cabinet for the nappy bucket and a changing table with a curtain front blend right in with this bathroom's traditional style.

soap opera

Sturdy, slip-resistant and portable, a baby bath can be used in the bath or a large sink. Use a handy caddy for toiletries and a cushion for your knees.

to each his own Organise a family bathroom by assigning each child a spot, and even a towel colour. Keep bath toys at the ready in baskets attached to the bath.

photo credits:

front cover Justin Bernhaut; **2–5** IPC Syndication/*Practical Parenting*; **6–7** Redcover.com; **13** Photozest/Inside/M Francken; **14** Pieter Estersohn; **16–17** Lisa Romerein; **18–19** Getty Images/Mark Lund; **20–21** Taverne Agency/John Dummer/production Yvonne Bakker; **22–23** Minh + Wass; **24–25** Photozest/Inside/B Claessens; **26–27** Redcover.com; **28–29** Alan Shortall; **30–31** Justin Bernhaut; **33** Alan Shortall; **34** Red Cover/Johnny Bouchier; **36–39** Pieter Estersohn; **40** Corbis/Beateworks/Scott Mayoral; **41** Alexander van Berge/*Eigen Huis & Interieur;* **42–43** Minh + Wass; **44–45** Justin Bernhaut; **46–47** IPC Syndication/*Ideal Home*/Simon Whitmore; **48–49** Lisa Romerein; **50–51** Photozest/Inside/L Wauman; **52** Taverne Agency/Hotze Eisma/production Anna Draijer; **53** Narratives/Kate Gadsby; **54–55** IPC Syndication/*Practical Parenting;* **58–59** Hotze Eisma; **61** Redcover.com; **66–67** Lisa Romerein; **68–69** IPC Syndication/*Practical Parenting;* **70–71** Photozest/Inside/L Wauman; **72–73** IPC Syndication/*Practical Parenting;* **74–75** IPC Syndication/*Homes & Gardens*/Polly Wreford; **78–79** Belle Maison; **80–81** Hotze Eisma; **82–83** Elizabeth Whiting & Associates (EWA Stock)/Lu Jeffery; **100** Eric Roth; **102–103** IPC Syndication/*Ideal Home*/Simon Whitmore; **105** Photozest/Inside/M Francken; **108–09** IPC Syndication/*Homes & Gardens*/Polly Wreford; **110** Minh + Wass; **118** Getty Images/Christopher Drake; **119** Getty Images/Ryan McVay; **123** Photozest/Inside/M Francken; **126** IPC Syndication/*Practical Parenting;* **128–129** Taverne Agency/Anne de Leeux/production Stephanie Rammeloo; **back cover (left)** Minh + Wass.

All other photography © Weldon Owen Inc./Pottery Barn: **1, 57, 62, 64–65, 76–77, 85–86, 88–99, 101, 106, 111–117, 120–121, 124, 127, 130–41, back cover (right)** Melanie Acevedo; **56, 142–143** David Matheson.

Special thanks to photography researchers Nadine Bazar and Sarah Airey.